The French and Indian War

by Peggy Caravantes

Content Consultant
C. Richard King, Professor of Comparative Ethnic Studies
Washington State University

CORE
LIBRARY

Published by ABDO Publishing Company, PO Box 398166, Minneapolis, MN 55439. Copyright © 2013 by Abdo Consulting Group, Inc.

Printed in the United States of America,
North Mankato, Minnesota
112012
012013

THIS BOOK CONTAINS AT LEAST 10% RECYCLED MATERIALS.

Editor: Blythe Hurley
Series Designer: Becky Daum

Cataloging-in-Publication Data
Caravantes, Peggy.
 The French and Indian War / Peggy Caravantes.
  p. cm. -- (Foundations of our nation)
Includes bibliographical references and index.
ISBN 978-1-61783-709-8
1. United States--History--French and Indian War, 1754-1763--Juvenile literature. I. Title.
973.2/6--dc22
                                        2012946492

Photo credits: North Wind/North Wind Picture Archives, cover, 1, 4, 9, 10, 14, 17, 20, 24, 27, 30, 32, 36, 40, 45; National Geographic/Getty Images, 12; Universal Images Group/Getty Images, 18, 34; Time Life Pictures/Getty Images, 22, Red Line Editorial, 39

Cover: The French surrendered Fort Louisburg to the British in 1758.

CONTENTS

CHAPTER ONE
Colonies and Conflicts 4

CHAPTER TWO
Seeking the Advantage 14

CHAPTER THREE
Great Britain
Heats Up the War 22

CHAPTER FOUR
The Campaign
against Quebec 30

CHAPTER FIVE
Consequences of the
French and Indian War 36

Important Dates 42

Stop and Think 44

Glossary 46

Learn More 47

Index 48

About the Author 48

Colonies and Conflicts

During the 1500s, European countries began creating colonies in distant parts of the world. Great Britain, France, and Spain were claiming land in the Americas and Asia. This new land brought wealth and power. By the 1600s, Great Britain and France were fighting over land in North America.

American Indians traded beaver pelts with white traders. Fur was an important source of wealth.

Land Grabbing

French colonists settled in New France throughout the 1600s. This area stretched from present-day eastern Canada to the Great Lakes and down into the Mississippi River Valley. People from Great Britain settled along the Atlantic coast. Slowly settlers spread into the Ohio River Valley.

Here, the Allegheny and Monongahela Rivers join to form the Ohio River. These three rivers were important trade routes. They provided a path to the West. The nation that controlled the rivers would control the valley.

The Iroquois American Indians lived in this valley. But white settlers still forced them out many times. The American Indians formed alliances with both the British and the French in return for trade goods.

The struggle over this land was connected to ongoing conflict between Great Britain and France. This resulted in the Seven Years' War.

Conflicting Claims

The French and Indian War was not between France and the American Indians. It was between Great Britain and France for control of this new land and the lands that lay beyond. American Indians played an important role as allies on both sides.

Colonial Resources

New land was called a colony. During the 1700s, European nations fought for resources in these new colonies. The most important trade was in furs. France made agreements with American Indian nations to buy furs. Great Britain wanted to buy furs as well. This was one reason for the French and Indian War.

Some British colonists believed the land in the Ohio River Valley was theirs. A group of rich Virginia businessmen called the Ohio Company had claimed much of the area in 1749. The American Indians in Ohio had given them permission to build a storehouse with military defenses there. Great Britain wanted more farmland for new British settlers.

The French also believed the land belonged to them. Robert de La Salle had claimed it for France earlier in the 1600s. The French wanted to use the land to expand their fur trade westward. They built a series of forts along the edge of the valley to protect their claim.

The governor of Virginia sent men to construct Fort Prince George in early 1754. He wanted to protect Great Britain's claim to the Ohio River Valley. The British hoped the fort would serve as a starting point for British settlement. But the French military drove the British away and continued building the fort themselves in April. They renamed it Fort Duquesne.

The governor of Virginia did not know the fort had been lost to the French. He sent more men to finish building it. Among them was George Washington. He was a 21-year-old major in the Virginia militia. When the group's commander died suddenly, Washington took charge. Soon afterward, he heard the French had taken over the fort.

French explorer Robert de la Salle's travels helped
France claim large parts of North America.

Major George Washington commands troops during the French and Indian War.

Washington's group surprised a French scouting party not far from Fort Duquesne. He and his men attacked. All of the French were either killed or captured in the battle that followed.

Fort Necessity

Other French forces in the area fought back against the British. Washington and his men quickly built a wooden structure made of upright posts to protect themselves. Only approximately 60 men fit inside. Many of them were too weak and ill to fight. They named the structure Fort Necessity. But Washington's soldiers could not resist the French attack. He was quickly forced to surrender. Washington agreed to leave two of his men at Fort Duquesne to guarantee the British would not attack again. His defeat led the colonies to seek Great Britain's help to fight the French.

Alliances

Both the British and the French wanted alliances with American Indian nations. The British allied with the

A modern re-creation of Fort Necessity, where Washington was forced to surrender to French forces during the French and Indian War

Iroquois. Their villages stretched across upper New York and into Ontario. The French's many American Indian allies disliked each other. But they hated the

Iroquois even more. Despite these alliances, the American Indian nations distrusted both the French and the British. Both countries had already broken promises with American Indians or moved into their lands without permission.

EXPLORE ONLINE

The focus in Chapter One was on the factors in North America that led to the French and Indian War. The Web site below tracks the key events of the war and the ways in which it changed US history. Go to the timeline entry for 1753. How does this information differ from what you have read in this text? What differences were there in the points of view of the French, the British, and the American Indians?

French and Indian War Timeline: Explore the Fight for a Continent

www.wqed.org/tv/specials/the-war-that-made-america/timeline.html

CHAPTER TWO

Seeking the Advantage

Great Britain sent troops to the colonies in 1755. General Edward Braddock was chosen to lead them. Braddock faced a number of challenges. He had almost no battlefield experience. He did not have enough supplies or soldiers. And he did not want to work with the American Indians.

General Braddock was not prepared for the realities of warfare during the French and Indian War. His brutal defeat had serious consequences for British and colonial forces.

French Warfare

Braddock's goal was to take control of the Ohio River Valley. He led both British and colonial soldiers in an attempt to take Fort Duquesne back. The British would control the valley if they could control that fort. But the French and their American Indian allies were more familiar with the area. They also used a different style of warfare. They used surprise attacks and fought from behind rocks and trees.

Braddock was not used to this different kind of war. The French surprised Braddock's soldiers near Fort Duquesne. He kept them moving in straight lines. He refused to let his

The Seven Years' War

The Seven Years' War (1756–1763) has been called the first real world war. France and Great Britain fought for control of colonies in Europe, Central America, Africa, Asia, and North America. In North America, the war was called the French and Indian War. This war was important to the colonists because victory would allow them to continue spreading westward.

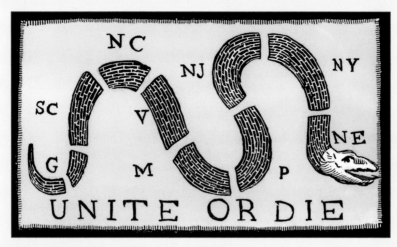

America's First Political Cartoon
Benjamin Franklin drew this cartoon after the Albany Congress in 1754. That was a meeting where representatives from each of the colonies met with members of the Iroquois to try to reach an agreement to fight the French together. It is also a map of the colonies during the French and Indian War. Which colonies are represented in the picture? Why might the snake be cut into pieces?

men take cover among the trees. His troops were overcome by the other soldiers. Close to 1,000 British soldiers were wounded or died. Braddock himself was wounded and died four days later.

French Success

General Braddock's defeat caused problems for the British forces. The French captured supplies, weapons, and ammunition. They also found Braddock's battle

Mortally wounded, General Braddock retreats from the Monongahela River with his men.

plans and a map of Fort Duquesne he had. The British had no idea their plans had been discovered.

War Declared

By 1756, British and French troops had been attacking each other's forts for two years. Most of the victories had gone to the French. French actions against the British in other parts of the world finally pushed the British to declare war on May 18. France declared war on Great Britain on June 9. The French and Indian War had officially begun.

Both sides chose new leaders after declaring war. Lord Loudoun became the British commander in chief in North America. The Marquis de Montcalm became French commander. He had many

Captain Stobo's Map

Robert Stobo was one of the soldiers Washington left behind at Fort Duquesne. He is remembered for drawing a map of the fort while he was there. Stobo smuggled the map out to the British. He was sentenced to death by beheading at his trial by French forces. But he escaped with other Americans in a canoe down the Saint Lawrence River before the punishment could be carried out.

General Braddock marches through the wilderness to Fort Duquesne.

years of military experience but was not ready for wilderness warfare. Still, his victories early in the war were encouraging. French troops and their American Indian allies spread fear by attacking the British settlements. Many British attacks on the French ended in defeat.

Adoption into an American Indian Nation

This passage, from *An account of the remarkable occurrences in the life and travels of Col. James Smith*, describes his adoption ceremony into an American Indian tribe.

> *The day after my arrival a number of Indians collected about me, and one of them began to pull the hair out of my head . . . he went on, as if he had been plucking a turkey, until he had all the hair clean out of my head, except a small spot about three or four inches square on my crown. This they cut off with a pair of scissors, excepting three locks, which they dressed up in their own mode. . . . After this they bored my nose and ears, and fixed me up with earrings and nose jewels. They ordered me . . . to put on a breechclout. Then they painted my head, face and body in various colors. They put a large belt of wampum on my neck, and silver bands on my hands and right arm, and so an old chief led me out into the street.*
>
> Source: Cave, Alfred A. The French and Indian War. Westport, CT: Greenwood Press, 2004. Print. 136.

What's the Big Idea?

Take a look at Smith's experience with the American Indians. What is his main idea? What evidence supports his point? Come up with a few sentences showing how Smith uses two or three pieces of evidence to support his main point.

CHAPTER THREE

Great Britain Heats Up the War

William Pitt became secretary of state in Great Britain in December 1756. He believed the American colonies were very important. Getting France out of North America became an important concern. In order to win the war, British forces would need to capture French colonial cities. But this would not be easy.

William Pitt, the secretary of state of Great Britain, was determined to beat France in the war.

After the Fort William Henry surrender, the American Indians attacked the wounded and sick British soldiers in an unexpected massacre.

The Siege of Fort William Henry

French leader Montcalm targeted Fort William Henry during the summer of 1757. This was near Montreal. The British forces there did not have enough troops or supplies. They surrendered after a six-day siege.

American Indians were usually paid by the French for taking the belongings of the British soldiers. This time Montcalm said the British would take their belongings with them. This angered the American Indians. They felt Montcalm was breaking his agreement.

Recapturing the Forts

Pitt was determined to beat France. By 1758, he ordered 50,000 British soldiers and colonial militia to prepare to fight.

Pitt chose General Jeffrey Amherst to lead the attack on Fort Louisbourg, near Quebec, Canada. Victory there would give the British control of all boat traffic in and out of Quebec and the rest of Canada.

A large group of French soldiers hid in trenches behind a barrier of trees. After a brief battle, the French troops fled toward the fort. The British attack on the

Smallpox

When the American Indians attacked the British soldiers after the Fort William Henry surrender, they didn't realize the British were sick with smallpox. Smallpox is a deadly disease. Large numbers of American Indians also became sick with the disease and died. Those who survived had pit-like scars from the blisters that formed on their skin. Eventually a shot was developed that protects people against smallpox.

French lasted seven weeks. The French surrendered on July 27.

The next British target was Fort Frontenac. This was next to Lake Ontario. It was an important spot for fur trade, the source of New France's wealth. This battle lasted one day before the French soldiers surrendered. The British did not lose any men in the battle.

General John Forbes decided the next target would be Fort Duquesne. He would not repeat Braddock's earlier mistakes. He would make sure to have a place where his men could retreat when attacked.

The British also needed more American Indian allies. Forbes turned to German-born missionary Christian Frederick Post for help. Post had built relationships with several American Indian nations. On October 26, he met with members of those nations. The agreement was called the Treaty of Easton. It promised to give the American Indians back

American Indian allies were important to both sides of the conflict during the French and Indian War.

their land around the Ohio River Valley. It also agreed to give back other territorial rights if they joined the British. These promises were never kept.

The outlook was not good for the French at Fort Duquesne. The men were low on food and other supplies. Many supplies had been lost at Fort Frontenac. On November 24, while the British were still ten miles away, the French commander and his men retreated. But first they completely destroyed the fort.

Fort Niagara by Lake Erie was the next British target. Feeling the British forces were now likely to win, almost 1,000 Iroquois joined the British troops. The French leader sent out messengers with an urgent plea for help. Assistance arrived on July 23. With help in place, the French attacked the next morning. The British held their fire until the French reached the British ditches. They then attacked the enemy. The French surrendered on July 25.

This defeat ended the French attempt to retake the Ohio River Valley. It also marked the end of French dominance in the war.

Post's Address to the American Indians

Post's goal in the Treaty of Easton was to convince the American Indians to leave their French allies and side with the British. Post was sincere in his speech. Great Britain was not:

> *Every one who lays hold of the belt of peace, I proclaim peace to them from the English nation, and let you know that the great King of England does not incline to have war with Indians, but he wants to live in peace and love with them, if they will lay down the hatchet and leave off war against him. . . .*
>
> *We look upon you as our countrymen, that sprung out of the same ground with us . . . we think, therefore, that it is our duty to take care of you, and we in brotherly love advise you to come away with your whole nation, and as many friends as you can get.*
>
> Source: Cave, Alfred A. The French and Indian War. Westport, CT: Greenwood Press, 2004. Print. 136.

Consider Your Audience

Review this passage. Consider how you would change it for a different audience, such as your parents or friends. Write a blog post conveying the same information for the new audience. Write it so they can understand it. What is the best way to get your point across? How does your approach differ from the original text, and why?

CHAPTER FOUR

The Campaign against Quebec

British victory in the French and Indian War was near. Only Quebec remained to be conquered. It was a walled city on high cliffs and the gateway to New France. A British victory would cut off Montcalm's communication with French forces. It would also cut off his troops' supplies.

Brigadier General James Wolfe was confident as he led his ships up the Saint Lawrence River toward

The British captured Quebec during the Battle of the Plains of Abraham.

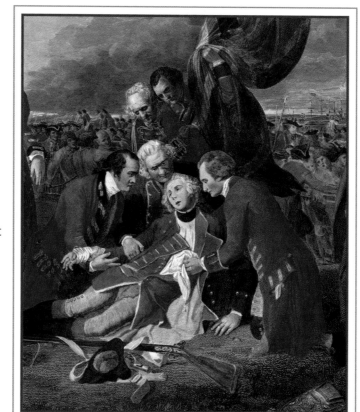

General Wolfe died after the battle on the Plains of Abraham. He became a folk hero and was the subject of numerous stories, poems, and songs.

French Surrender

The French tried to take Quebec back in 1760 but failed. British troops attacked the city of Montreal. The remaining sick or injured French were housed there. The French were helpless against the British forces. On September 8, the French surrendered Montreal. This meant they also surrendered all of Canada.

The French and Indian War officially ended with the signing of the Treaty of Paris on February 10, 1763. This treaty gave Canada and all French-held territory east of the Mississippi except New Orleans to Great Britain. France gave up its colonial claims in India and all of Canada except for two small islands. Great Britain took Florida from Spain. These terms left France with little power or land in North America and made Great Britain a world empire.

FURTHER EVIDENCE

British victory in the French and Indian War depended on conquering Quebec. Review Chapter Four. Identify its main point and find supporting evidence. Then visit the following Web sites to learn more about the war and to find a quote that supports the chapter's main point.

The French and Indian War

www.ushistory.org/us/8b.asp

www.shmoop.com/french-indian-war/war.html

CHAPTER FIVE

Consequences of the French and Indian War

Fighting between the French and British was over. But relations between the British and their American Indian allies were tense. The American Indians were angry about what they saw as broken British promises. The British tried to create a more lasting peace by carrying out the promises of the Treaty of Easton. They banned colonists from settling beyond the Appalachian Mountains.

Chief Pontiac and his Native American allies visited British forces during Pontiac's War, when American Indians fought back against the British.

Chief Pontiac's Address

On May 5, 1763, Ottawa Chief Pontiac called on other American Indian leaders to join him in attacking Fort Detroit due to what he saw as broken British promises. Within two months, several forts had been taken or destroyed. Pontiac gave a speech during this gathering, saying:

> It is important for us, my brothers, that we exterminate from our lands this nation which seeks only to destroy us. . . . The English sell us goods twice as dear as the French do, and their goods do not last. Scarcely have we bought a blanket or something else to cover ourselves with before we must think of getting another. . . .

But this did not calm the American Indians. It also upset colonists who had been waiting to move westward.

The land the colonists had won would encourage them to have a special vision about their country and its future. This led to a century of conflict between settlers and American Indians as the young United States slowly but surely spread west.

The Road to Revolution

Great Britain spent huge amounts of money during

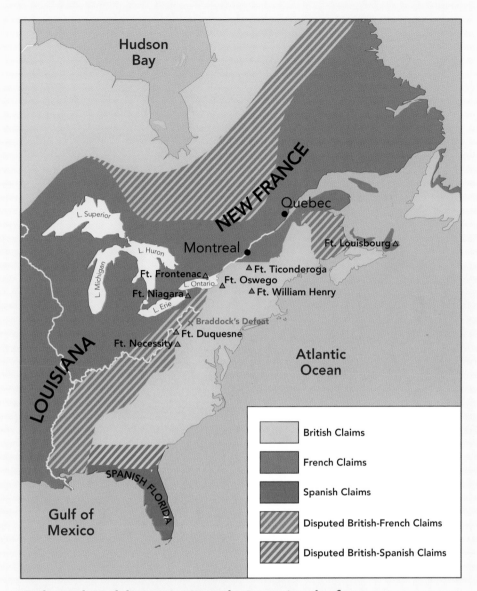

Map labels:
Hudson Bay
L. Superior
L. Huron
L. Michigan
L. Ontario
L. Erie
NEW FRANCE
Quebec
Montreal
Ft. Louisbourg △
Ft. Frontenac △
△ Ft. Ticonderoga
Ft. Oswego △
Ft. Niagara △
△ Ft. William Henry
LOUISIANA
✗ Braddock's Defeat
△ Ft. Duquesne
Ft. Necessity △
Atlantic Ocean
SPANISH FLORIDA
Gulf of Mexico

Legend:
British Claims
French Claims
Spanish Claims
Disputed British-French Claims
Disputed British-Spanish Claims

Colonial Holdings in North America before the French and Indian War

This map shows the land in North America held by Great Britain, France, and Spain before the French and Indian War. What does the map show about the division of the land before the war? Based upon what you read in the text, how did these divisions change after the Treaty of Paris was signed?

Settlers move into the Ohio Territory.

the war. It also supported a global empire. The British government decided to tax the colonies to help raise money. But the colonists believed the right to tax should come from the approval of the citizens. For the next ten years, the colonists became more and more angry about Great Britain's attempts to control the colonies and to raise money through taxes. For the first time, they began to think of themselves as a unit instead of 13 individual governments. Together they protested taxes, limits on westward expansion, and other British laws. These protests lit the spark that would start the Revolutionary War in 1775.

IMPORTANT DATES

1749

The British and French both claim land in the Ohio River Valley.

1754

The Albany Congress meets in June.

1754

George Washington surrenders Fort Necessity.

1758

The British have victories at Forts Louisbourg and Frontenac.

1758

The British and several American Indian nations sign the Treaty of Easton.

1759

The Battle on the Plains of Abraham for Quebec takes place in September.

1755

Great Britain sends troops to North America to support the war effort.

1756

Great Britain and France declare war on each other as part of the Seven Years' War.

1757

The French have victories at Fort William Henry.

1760

The French surrender Montreal and all of Canada.

1763

Chief Pontiac leads the American Indian rebellion against the British.

1763

The signing of the Treaty of Paris on February 10 ends the French and Indian War.

Take a Stand

This book discusses how the British and the French treated various American Indian nations. Take a position on this issue, and write a short essay explaining your opinion. Include your reasons for your opinion, and give some facts and details to support those reasons.

Dig Deeper

What questions do you still have about the French and Indian War? Do you want to learn more about the weapons used at the time or the Europeans' American Indian allies and their way of life? Write down one or two questions that can guide you in doing research. With an adult's help, find a few reliable new sources about this time period that can help answer your questions. Write a few sentences about how you did your research and what you learned from it.

You Are There

Imagine you are living in Quebec during Brigadier General James Wolfe's attempt to capture the city. Write 300 words describing your experience. How do you feel about the decisions made by Wolfe during the course of the struggle?

Tell the Tale

This book discusses how Great Britain angered the colonists after the end of the French and Indian War. Write 200 words that tell the true tale of how the colonists felt. Be sure to set the scene, develop a sequence of events, and offer a conclusion.

GLOSSARY

alliance
a formal union between nations

ammunition
explosive military items

artillery
large mounted guns

civilians
persons not serving in the armed forces

dominance
having the most influence or control

massacre
the savage killing of a large number of people

reinforcements
military units sent to strengthen troops already gathered

siege
surrounding of a fort or town by an army intent on capturing it

surrender
to give up the power or control upon demand

LEARN MORE

Books

Pederson, Charles E. *The French & Indian War*. Edina, MN: ABDO Publishing Company, 2010.

Santella, Andrew. *The French and Indian War*. New York: Scholastic, 2011.

Todish, Timothy J. *America's First World War, The French and Indian War, 1754–1763*. New York: Purple Mountain, 2002.

Web Links

To learn more about the French and Indian War, visit ABDO Publishing Company online at **www.abdopublishing.com**. Web sites about the war are featured on our Book Links page. These links are routinely monitored and updated to provide the most current information available.

Visit **www.mycorelibrary.com** for free additional tools for teachers and students.

INDEX

alliances, 6, 7, 11–13, 16, 20, 26, 29, 37

Amherst, Jeffrey, 25

Braddock, Edward, 15, 16–18, 26, 39

broken promises, 13, 24, 27, 37, 38

colonial holdings, 39

Duquesne, Fort, 8, 11, 16, 18, 19, 26–27, 39

Forbes, John, 26

forts, 8, 11, 24, 25, 28, 38, 39

Frontenac, Fort, 26–27, 39

fur trade, 7, 8, 26

Great Lakes, 6, 39

Iroquois, 6, 12–13, 17, 28

Loudoun, Lord, 19

Montcalm, Marquis de, 19, 24, 31–33

Montreal, 24, 34, 39

New France, 6, 26, 31, 39

Ohio Company, 7

Ohio River, 6

Ohio River Valley, 6, 7–8, 16, 27, 28

Pitt, William, 23, 25

Plains of Abraham, 33

Pontiac, Chief, 38

Post, Christian Frederick, 26, 29

Quebec, 25, 31–33, 34, 35, 39

Revolutionary War, 41

Saint Lawrence River, 19, 31–32, 33

Salle, Robert de La, 8

Seven Years' War, 6, 16

smallpox, 25

Smith, James, 21

Stobo, Robert, 19

Treaty of Easton, 26, 29, 37

Treaty of Paris, 35, 39

warfare, 16–17, 20

Washington, George, 8, 11, 19

Wolfe, James, 31, 32–33

ABOUT THE AUTHOR

A retired educator living in San Antonio, Texas, Peggy Caravantes is the author of 11 middle grade and young adult biographies. She enjoys reviewing her books in school settings and presenting writing workshops to middle school students.